TRACK & FIELD

By Mark Littleton

ZondervanPublishingHouse
Grand Rapids, Michigan

A Division of HarperCollins*Publishers*

Track and Field
Copyright © 1995 by Mark Littleton

Requests for information should be addressed to:
Zondervan Publishing House
Grand Rapids, Michigan 49530

Library of Congress Cataloging-in-Publication Data

Littleton, Mark R., 1950–
        Track and field / Mark Littleton.
            p. cm. –– (Sports heroes)
        Includes bibliographical references.
        ISBN: 0-310-49581-4 (softcover)
        1. Track and field athletes—Biography—Juvenile literature. 2.
Track and field athletes—Religious life—Juvenile literature. [1.
Track and field athletes. 2. Christian life.] I. Title. II. Series: Little-
ton, Mark R., 1950–   Sports heroes.
GV697.A1L59 1995
796.42'092'2–dc20   94–44892
[B]   CIP
                                                                        AC

Edited by Tom Raabe
Interior design by Joe Vriend

Printed in the United States of America
95 96 97 98 99 00 / ❖ DC / 10 9 8 7 6 5 4 3 2 1

To James and Liz Taylor—
keep the flame alive.

Contents

Champions for Christ

Track and field includes a multitude of different events and competitions. Most people specialize in one event. Either they're sprinters or long distance runners, discus throwers or pole vaulters, or experts in one of any number of other means to show off ability, endurance, muscle, and guts.

In this book, you'll meet six athletes who have excelled in their events for many years. They have proven they have what it takes to achieve high honors in the halls of sport. All of them are champions. All of them are Christians. All of them serve first their Lord, and second their craft.

Admire them. Learn from them. They're people of whom the Lord himself says, "Well done, good and faithful servant."

Chapter 1

Height: 5 feet, 9 inches

Born: January 16, 1902, in Tientsin, China

Died: February 21, 1945, Wiehsien Internment Camp, China

Track events: 100 meters, 200 meters, 400 meters, relays

College: Edinburgh University, Scotland

Eric Liddell: The Flying Scotsman

It was the 1924 Olympics, and the men had taken their places for the 400 meters. Before the race, Eric Liddell, a Christian, had received a short note from his athletics masseur. It read, "In the old book it says, 'He that honors me, I will honor.' Wishing you the best of success always." Liddell went on to run a race of races, a race that would go down in history.

Why was the outcome of that particular race so special? Because it wasn't Liddell's best event. He had been world-ranked in the 100 meters, but he had dropped out of that event because the heats were run on a Sunday. Liddell believed he should follow the Fourth Commandment: "You shall remember the Sabbath and keep it holy." But how could he do this—to himself, to Britain, to the world? It was like shooting yourself in the foot before running a marathon. Everyone wanted to see him compete in the 100, but it was not to be.

The British organizers still wanted to run Liddell in something, though; he was famous all over Scotland. So they settled on two other events: the 200 and the 400 meters. Many felt that having Liddel run only these races was a concession—Liddell would never win. Almost no one remembered that Someone else was watching over the races as well. Who? God himself! And God had been watching Eric run for a long time.

Eric was born in Tientsin, China, on January 16, 1902, to missionary parents. Something called the Boxer Rebellion was raging in China at that time, and thousands of Christians and hundreds of missionaries were being murdered. The Liddell family had barely escaped to Shanghai and then Tientsin.

Eric was the second son of the Liddell family, and he gained a sister and another brother in the next few years. When he was five, the Liddells came home to Scotland on a furlough. His father went back to China in 1908, but Eric and his brothers and sister remained in London, England, to attend school. Eric would not see China again until 1937 when he went back as a missionary.

Eric excelled in sports. "I don't think much of lessons," he said, "but I can run."[1] He could, too, even though he possessed a strange running style. He'd flail and churn his arms in the air with his head tilted all the way back as if he were looking at something high in the sky. But even though he couldn't see where he was going, he still won. Eric and his brother dominated sports in their high school, Eltham College (some high schools in the British system are called colleges). They both held records in the long jump, 100 yards, cross-country, high jump, quarter mile, and hurdles. Eric's time of 10.2 seconds in the 100-yard dash is still a school record.

After high school, Eric studied basic science at Edinburgh University, one of Scotland's greatest universities, and soon got involved in running. On one occasion, he lost a heat of the 100 to a high-rated sprinter named G. Innes Stewart. In the final, though, Eric won. And in the 220, Stewart beat Eric by only inches. It was the only race Liddell ever lost in his whole Scottish running career!

In no time, Eric was winning everywhere. In 1922 he won three titles at the Inter-Universities Sports Meet: the 100, 220, and 440. He won the 100 and 220 in the 1922 Scottish Championships, and repeated in both every year until 1925, a record that has never been topped.

In the 1923 Inter-Universities Sports he broke three records: the 100 in 10.1 seconds, the 220 in 21.6, and the 440 in 50.2. The 440 record remained on the books till 1957. Eric was bringing home trophies and prizes from all over the world. At the same time, he was also considered a major rugby player and champion.

All during this time, Eric's faith was forming. He had always believed in God, having been taught early on by his parents about Christian living and faith. His was a simple, personal, unhurried faith. He saw faith as linked to his future. He had few doubts, if any, and considered going into missionary service early on. He always kept Sunday as a day of rest— he never ran or played sports on a Sunday—and felt it was the Lord's Day, a holy day to worship and serve God.

Eric's faith overflowed into his sports life too. In those days, everyone lined up equally at the start of a race. There was no "staggering" of the lanes as there is today. Runners had to fight for the inside rail after the gun went off. Neil Campbell, his opponent in one race, an inferior runner, was surprised when Eric gave him the inside lane. He wrote, "No athlete has ever made a bigger impact on people all over the world, and the description of him as 'the most famous, the most popular, and best-loved athlete Scotland has ever produced' is no exaggeration."[2]

Eric was also a man of character and love. On one occasion, he walked up to a black opponent and talked with him freely when all the others avoided the man. He always offered to lend his trowel to other runners as they "dug in" for the start (starting blocks would not be used until 1927). He shook hands before a race and was always friendly and encouraging. No one looked upon him, though, as some kind of do-gooder; it was just the natural over-flow of his personality. He liked people, and he enjoyed running. Why not bring the two together and make it fun for all?

As the Olympics of 1924 neared, everyone won-dered which athletes would be chosen to represent Great Britain. Eric had never raced in London and was still unknown in much of England. However, the 1923 AAA Championships in London changed all that. Eric ran with his wild arms flailing and charmed the crowd. More than that, he set a new British record of 9.7 seconds in the 100, a record that stood until 1958 and remains one of the longest-standing records in British history. Eric also won the 220 in 21.6 seconds, not a record, but a tremen-dous showing.

If that didn't clinch it, then Eric's performance the following week at Stoke-on-Trent did. He won all three events: the 100, the 220, and the 440. The 440 was especially exciting because three strides into the race, J. J. Gillies of England knocked Eric off the track! Eric fell, stunned, wondering if he was disqualified. But he saw the officials motion him, so he got up and took off after the other runners, who were a good twenty yards beyond and two seconds ahead of him. Soon he caught up to fourth place, ten yards behind Gillies. With what looked like superhuman effort, he pushed even harder. With forty yards to go, he was only a third of the way there. But Eric wasn't going to quit. With more gargantuan strides, he caught up, then beat Gillies by two seconds. His time was 51.2 seconds, close to the record. He collapsed onto the field in exhaustion. As he was carried away, the crowd roared! Many said it was the greatest track running they had ever seen in their lives.

Eric ran literally on trust. It was as if he trusted God himself to get him to the finish line. Even though his style seemed to do everything to hold him back, Eric was propelled forward like a man possessed— or should we say, inspired! How did he do it? He said, "The first half I run as fast as I can, and the second half I run faster with God's help."[3]

There was another reason too. "I don't like to be beaten," said Eric. One author writes, "That explains the set of his teeth, the way he fought the air, the determination to stretch his body to the limits, the grit that took him off the ground when he fell and hurled himself to the finish line."[4]

Perhaps it was all part of Eric's joy and faith in Christ. He ran with abandon, as if no one but he and God were involved. As he said in the movie *Chariots of Fire*, "When I run, I feel his [God's] pleasure."

Eric was selected to run the 100 and the 200 meters in the Olympics. In the 100, he was the British champion. It was the greatest event, the "jewel" of the Games. Eric burned to win it.

And then he found out that the heats were to be held on a Sunday.

Eric's answer to the news was simply, "I'm not running." No doubt. No hashing it out. No back and forth. A simple no was all he said. Sunday was God's Day. He would not run on a Sunday, even if it was the Olympics.

Eric made his feelings clear the moment the news of the timetables came out. Those who knew him well, and his faith, were not surprised. Eric's decision was completely "in character." But few understood his stand, even Christians. Britain was horrified. They had pinned all their hopes on Liddell. It was as if the man wanted to lose everything!

17

The press came down on him too, some of them calling him a "traitor" to his country. The 100 was the blue-ribbon event of the Games, and this "fanatic" named Liddell was throwing it away on a matter of theological debate!

Nonetheless, many athletes supported Liddell. In fact, Tom Riddell, the leading British miler from 1925–35, once refused to run on a Sunday in Italy. It was Eric's influence that touched him.

But Eric was not turning down only the 100 meters. He also refused to run in the 4 x 100 and the 4 x 400 relays, because they were also run on a Sunday. His decision was regarded as athletic suicide. The only other British hope for the 100 meters was Harold Abrahams, whose best time had been roundly destroyed by the reigning Olympic champion, American Charles Paddock. Paddock had returned to the 1924 Games after winning in 1920.

What was there to do?

The best the Olympic committee could offer Eric was the 400 meters (in addition to the 200). It was far from Eric's best event, although he'd proved many times he could run it. The 400 is one of the most demanding races there is. You have to sprint the whole way, and the human body is not made for sprinting that distance. The 100 and 200 are natural sprints, but not the 400. The 400 requires the stamina of middle-distance running with the speed of the short, all-out events. It was not the "jewel" that the 100 was, either. And Eric had never really trained for the 400; he ran it simply because he liked to compete.

Later, Eric's wife said, "Eric always said that the great thing for him was that when he stood by his principles and refused to run in the 100 meters, he found that the 400 meters was really his race. He said he would never have known that otherwise. He would never have dreamed of trying the 400 meters at the Olympics."[5]

Eric wasn't sure he could win—not in the Olympics anyway. Britain's hopes for winning the 400 were in another runner, Guy Butler. However, Guy had a bad leg and could not start from the crouching position. There was little hope that Britain could capture a gold in the 400.

The Olympics that year were big, blustery, and bombastic. They opened on July 5, 1924, in Paris. Forty-four nations were represented, with over 3,000 participants—the biggest Olympics ever at that point. Johnny Weissmuller, who would win three golds in swimming, was there. He would later become a film star as the legendary "Tarzan" and make many movies about that jungle hero.

Above all, it was hot. The stadium was like a furnace. In the 10,000 meters, runners dropped from pure heat exhaustion. Only 23 of 38 starters finished the race.

Eric was constantly pressured to rethink his stand against running on Sunday. He even confided to a friend that he doubted he was right. But he stuck to it. He would honor the Lord's Day.

What *did* Eric do that Sunday? He preached at a Scots church in another part of Paris. No one remembers what he spoke about; Eric was only an average speaker. But many people came to hear this man who had taken a stand for his faith.

On Monday, Eric arrived at the stadium in time to see Harold Abrahams win the 100 meters for Britain in 10.6 seconds, an Olympic record. The gold changed Abrahams' life. He went from being an obscure runner to a hero, and later became a "dean of sports" in Britain, achieving renown in broadcasting and journalism.

On Wednesday, Eric won a bronze in the 200 meters. But there was little said about it in the news. With all the publicity of Eric's refusal to run on a Sunday, no one seemed to notice his stout showing in the 200 meters.

Then came the 400 heats on Thursday. Eric did fine, 50.2 seconds, but placed well behind the leader. Later on the same day he won his quarterfinal heat with a personal best of 49.0. The next day in the semifinals he got his time down to 48.2. He was getting better and better.

However, in the other semifinal Horatio Fitch flashed around the track in 47.8, destroying both the

Olympic and world records. Two other men came in with better times than Eric. He was not the favorite.

Finally, the day of the finals arrived: Friday, July 11, 1924. It was as he was getting ready for this last race that Eric received the note from his masseur. "He that honors me, I will honor," the note reminded Eric.

Six men lined up to run in that furnace-hot stadium that morning: two Britishers, two Americans, a Swiss, and a Canadian. Customarily, Eric walked about shaking hands. He had drawn the worst possible position: the sixth lane on the outside.

Suddenly, as the men got ready to start, there was a blast of Scottish bagpipes. The Cameron Highlanders, a military outfit at the Games, had burst into music! They marched around the stadium in full dress, kilts and all. No one could stop them. They were there to show support for their brother, Eric Liddell, in the outside lane.

Finally, the bagpipes stopped. The runners crouched, ready. At the gun, Eric set off at a blistering pace. He ran the first 200 meters in just .6 seconds over Jackson Scholz's winning 200-meter time days before. Eric was in full sprint and stride. No one thought he could keep it up: rigor mortis would set in at 300 meters.

But he had not even thrown his head back yet!

The runners came off the bend into the straightaway. And then it happened. Eric should have been dying, but instead, he seemed to be carried along on a power unseen. He stepped up the pace. His head fell back, his mouth dropped open, his knees leaped, and his arms flailed. He began increasing his lead over the nearest contender.

Liddell was flying! Almost literally.

The crowd was on its feet roaring. It was quite a spectacle. No one had ever seen a human run like this, much less win. The track seemed to be in flames.

Liddell hit the tape five meters ahead of Fitch, who came in second. His time was 47.6 seconds, an Olympic record. The cheering throughout the stadium was deafening. The race became the "glamour" win of the 1924 Games. Liddell had honored his Lord Jesus Christ, and his Lord Jesus Christ had now honored him.

Instantly, Liddell was a world personality. Clubs would be started in his name. All of Scotland, some of whom had called him a traitor, now saw him as a hero. Eric went on to become a missionary to China, and in 1945 he died of a brain tumor in a Japanese internment camp. As the movie *Chariots of Fire* said in its last frame: "All of Scotland mourned."

One day we who believe in Jesus will see Eric Liddell in heaven. Maybe he'll even run for us!

1. Sally Magnuson, *The Flying Scot* (New York: Quartet Books, 1981), 24.
2. Magnuson, 35.
3. Magnuson, 38.
4. Magnuson, 38.
5. Magnuson, 45.

Chapter 2

★ Jim Ryun ★

Height: 6 feet, 3 inches

Weight: 160 pounds

Born: April 29, 1947

Track events: Mile, 1500 meters, 800 meters

College: University of Kansas

Jim Ryun: Going for the Gold

World-record-setting miler Jim Ryun always wanted to be someone important. In fact, *Superman* was one of his favorite TV programs during his elementary-school years in the 1950s. One day after watching the show, Jim went to the kitchen and mixed himself a special concoction of everything in the kitchen cabinet and refrigerator: dill-pickle juice, Coke, mustard, ketchup, orange juice, leftover chicken gravy, milk, iced tea, vinegar, and

Worcestershire sauce. He still wasn't satisfied, though, so he dumped in pepper, spices, and cayenne—nearly everything he could find. Then he took a long swallow from the glass.

Yuck! But he didn't throw up. He stood on the porch and leaped, expecting to fly.

Nothing happened.

Stumbling onto the lawn, he wondered what was wrong. Maybe he hadn't drunk enough. He went back to the porch and downed the rest of the horrible concoction. Once more he lifted his arms and prepared to fly.

He leaped . . . and fell down to the ground! Jim Ryun wasn't Superman and never would be. But he *would* go on to become one of the greatest mile runners of all time.

Jim didn't have an easy start with sports. At first he had his sights set on baseball, but in junior high and high school he was tall, gangly, and uncoordinated. After several failures in basketball and baseball, he decided to try track. When he discovered he wasn't very good at the hurdles and 50-yard dash, he gave the long jump and pole vault a try. But all he did was knock himself out. Finally he decided that the quarter mile—the long-distance run at his school—might be his event.

As a ninth grader in 1962, Jim lined up with the other kids to run the quarter mile. As the starter gun sounded, they all dashed down the track. At the halfway point, the death urge started to set into Jim's limbs. His heart pounded, he could barely breathe, and his legs became heavier and heavier. He chugged in at 58.5 seconds. Afterward, he crouched with his hands on his knees gasping for air. He almost decided to give up running.

But something inside Jim wanted to run that 440 again and maybe come in with a 52- or 53-seconds time. The next year he enrolled at Wichita (Kansas) East High School and decided to give track another try. Track did not begin till spring, however, so that fall he went out for cross-country—really long-distance running.

The first day of practice, after dressing in shorts and tennis shoes, the team headed out for a slow mile jog up to a local park. When they reached it, Jim thought it had been a nice practice; he was ready to go home. But after a few exercises, everyone got up and started jogging again. Everyone, that is, except Jim, who was lying down on the grass, ready for a snooze.

The coach's voice jarred him out of his day dreams. "Hey you, Ryun!" Jim turned to see the rest of the pack about 100 yards away. "Come on. We're gonna start the workout," the coach said.

Jim was amazed. *The workout wasn't over?*

Somehow he dragged himself to his feet and slogged off after the pack. The workout was murder: eight half-mile runs around the park. And the pack moved fast—they were no longer just jogging. After each loop, the group stopped, rested for a few moments, then started again.

By this time Jim was gagging. He couldn't get his breath. He sat out the next two runs, then tried another, and that was it for the day. How could he have possibly thought he could be a runner?

Several days later, Jim ran his first mile. He came in fourteenth with a time of 5:38. Even though his body felt like ground hamburger, he was improving. Despite the fact that even his parents encouraged him to give it up, Jim decided he liked track. He stuck with it.

The team had a race after each five days of workouts. As he kept with it, Jim's times continued to improve. He began to beat his teammates. Jim still hated the pain and the long, lonely workouts. He hated the driving slam of his feet on the pavement. But he loved running. Something about it made him feel free, happy, and significant. He finished the season with a new resolve.

The following spring, Jim went out for track once again. He says now that "when the Lord put together this body of mine, He put within it what can only be viewed as a number of remarkable uniquenesses."[1] Among those "uniquenesses" was an ability to endure pain; the power to stick with a hard, disciplined regimen; and an amazing kick in the last quarter of a mile.

In March, at the first track meet, Jim was pitted against juniors, seniors, and the state mile champion. He decided to simply try to keep up with the pack. No one told him he was supposed to go for the tape on his own during his last lap, so he followed the leader, state champion Charlie Harper, right to the tape! As he watched a replay of the race on the news that night, Jim realized he could have beaten the state champion. He was on his way! He had found his sport.

The following week, Jim had a chance to run against Harper again. This time he determined not to follow at the end, but to try to take the lead. He did exactly that, setting a meet mile record of 4 minutes, 26.4 seconds. He even made headlines in the *Wichita Eagle*, the newspaper he delivered each morning before school.

Jim's coach, Bob Timmons, was very excited. After watching Jim's development over the weeks, he decided to talk to Jim about his goals:

"What do you think you can do a mile in?" he said to the young runner.

"This year?" Jim replied. "Oh, I don't know, maybe—"

"Not this year," the coach interrupted. "I mean by the time you're a senior—ultimately."

Jim had never thought about it.

"I guess maybe 4:10," he said.

The coach shuffled some papers. "This is what I think," he said. "I've been keeping a chart of your performances." He pulled out a clipboard and showed Jim some numbers and lines. Then he said, "Do you see what I'm driving at?"

Jim couldn't speak.

"I'm talking about the four-minute mile, Jim. No high school boy has ever run one. I think you can be the first, if you're willing to go after it and work for it. I'm convinced you can do it."[2]

Jim was astonished. He didn't know much, but he knew enough to realize that a four-minute mile was a goal very few track greats had broken. But the coach wasn't joking. He had already handled several excellent milers, and he had confidence in his methods, even if Jim had little confidence in himself. Coach Timmons was sure that with the right combination of training, growth, commitment, and pure grit, Jim Ryun could be the first high school runner to break the incredible four-minute barrier.

He said to Jim, "You'll have to get used to people making fun of you and even ridiculing your efforts. For a boy with your uncertainty and reticent personality, that may be as hard as the workouts themselves. You're trying to do something nobody your age has ever tried before. I admit I don't know how my timetable will work out. We may have to adjust things as we go along. Neither of us will know until we get there. And that's the tough part, Jim. You'll be out there all by yourself. You're going to leave high school competition far behind."[3]

Jim continued racing. Many times Coach Timmons's eyeballs popped as he looked at his stopwatch after clocking Jim. By the end of his sophomore year, sixteen-year-old Jim had run a 4:08 mile. It was then that "Timmie," as the coach was called, gave public notice of Jim's goal. Some scoffed; others just watched. But Jim plugged away, posting better and better times.

At that time, Jim thought he was a Christian because he attended church regularly. However, he hadn't yet forged a personal, born-again relationship with Jesus. Because he had dedicated himself to running, Jim knew he'd have to decrease his involvement in his church. He was worried about what his pastor would think of that. But when Jim went to see him, his pastor told him, "If you don't set your goals high, you'll never reach them. If you're

going to go into this thing, a Christian ought to do his very best."[4]

It was all the encouragement Jim needed to push even harder toward his goal. During his junior year, nearly every workout included one long-distance run of fifteen to twenty miles. And that didn't even include the frequent "interval work," which meant running thirty or forty 440s and 880s in one afternoon, resting in between. In all, Jim was logging 110 miles a week, sixteen miles a day on average, much of it run under grueling weather conditions. But rain, shine, or snow, Jim plugged on.

There were many times when Jim wanted to give up. He found the constant pounding on the turf boring and painful. But always the coach brought him back to the goal. A four-minute mile wasn't something anyone could push him into. If Jim didn't want to do the work, there was no point. No one was going to browbeat him into performing.

Meets became routine as Jim took away all the honors. He was now ranked as one of the best milers in the country. In May, the real races began: the invitationals. Any amateur could enter these meets: from teenagers to those out of college. At the first invitational, the California Relays in Modesto, California, Jim would face three milers who had done 3:56 or better. Jim's best time at that point was 4:06. He'd never run in a race like this before, but he was there now. And he was ready.

When the gun went off, Jim settled into the back of the pack. The first lap went by pretty slowly in 63 seconds. Jim remained in last place after the second lap was completed in 1:05. Total time now: 2:05. Several people fell back and Jim passed them. By the end of the third lap he was in sixth place, running 3:06. The two leaders, Dyrol Burleson and Tom O'Hara, began to sprint and widened the lead. Jim was still back in the pack, but he was moving up.

Coming around the last corner, Jim ran for the tape for all he was worth. He passed into fifth, then fourth, and finally third place. At the finish it was Dyrol Burleson, first, in 4:00.2; Tom O'Hara, second, in 4:00.3; Jim Ryun, third, in 4:01.7.

It was an incredible finish. The crowd was on their feet, shouting and cheering. They knew that the guy in third was a high school kid. It was a tremendous showing, but it was not the four-minute mile Jim had wanted.

Then came the Compton Invitational in Los Angeles. Many of the runners from the California Relays were there. Coach Timmons advised Jim to go after it this time, not to hang back in the pack, but to go for a better position—maybe not the "pace" man, but third or fourth.

The gun sounded. Jim got a good start but was bumped early in the first lap. While someone with good balance might have recovered quickly, Jim had suffered a very high fever as an infant that damaged some of the nerves in his inner ear. He was left with 50-percent hearing loss as well as serious equilibrium and balance problems. Whenever he was jostled, he would lose his equilibrium and be very much off balance. When Jim was struck in the race, he didn't fall, but he *was* unsteady for a few seconds. He even went off the track and out of contention—for a moment.

Recovering, Jim jumped back onto the track and tore off after the others. He contented himself with the thought that he would probably be last place and kept on running. Then he heard his halfway time: 2:01.5—a record pace! He made it back to the pack, but when the sprint came on the fourth lap everyone took off ahead of him, and he wasn't able to catch up. He finished second to last.

Jim thought he'd run poorly, but a minute later it was announced that something never before seen in history had happened: eight men in a single race had finished under four minutes, Jim Ryun among them. His time was 3:59.0.

Coach Timmons and Jim were ecstatic. They had done it. A high school junior had run a sub-four-minute mile! It was an outstanding, unbelievable achievement. Jim had made his first mark on history.

Until then, Jim's times had not attracted more than local attention. But with the breaking of the four-minute mile, he achieved instant notoriety. His name and story were in *Time, Look, London Times,*

Teenage Christian, Junior Scholastic, Coronet, and *Amateur Athlete.* Jim was stunned and over-whelmed. He kept wondering if this was really happening to him.

Now that Jim had broken the four-minute barrier, there were other goals to be reached. First on the list was qualifying for the 1964 Olympics, which were to be held in Tokyo, Japan. Only the top three finishers in the Olympic time trials would go to Tokyo. Jim lived with Coach Timmons and his wife and family that summer, worked out on their farm, and did farm chores along with everyone else. Most of all, he trained for the Olympic time trials.

The day of the race came on September 13, 1964. Jim's picture had appeared on the cover of *Sports Illustrated* only days before. This was a 1500-meter run, not actually a mile, but a bit shorter. Still, the strategies and the basic endurance level remained the same.

The race started off slowly, with everyone bunched up. But by the time the runners had reached the last curve of the last lap, Jim had moved up into fifth place. A question popped into Jim's mind: should he go for it, or just finish in a decent spot? Instantly, something clicked. He'd worked so hard and for so long, why give up now? Suddenly, Jim was going for it, his kick in full stride. He moved into fourth place.

Burleson and O'Hara had opened a small gap and were in the lead. Jim Grelle, who had beaten Jim at Compton, was on the inside; Jim was on the outside. The four of them sprinted for the tape. Burleson was first. O'Hara was second. And it was Jim Ryun and Jim Grelle in third. Grelle lunged for the tape; Ryun met it in full sprint. Their times were the same—3:41.9—but the judges said Ryun had edged Grelle out. Jim was on his way to Tokyo.

Unfortunately, Jim was hit with a virus while he was in Tokyo. Though he made it through his first heat, he finished dead last in the semifinal. So much for Olympic glory.

Over time, however, Jim Ryun would achieve many remarkable moments. He would hold the world record several times, coming close to a 3:50 mile with a 3:51.1. He would go on to two more Olympics. In Mexico City in 1968, he would win the silver medal in the 1500, losing to Kip Keino, an African who won another gold and two silvers in two Olympics. In 1972, he went to Munich but was bumped and knocked off the track in the semifinals. He never caught up to the pack and finished in last place. Jim Ryun's quest for gold in the Olympics would never be realized. Even though various films showed that Jim was bumped, the judges wouldn't even look at them. Jim was never given another chance.

But something else also happened to Jim in 1972: He met Jesus Christ. It had been a long time coming, even though Jim had always considered himself a Christian. Through friends, coaches, and family, Jim was repeatedly confronted with people who spoke of knowing Jesus personally. Finally, one night he went to friends to ask them to pray for him. He was having trouble financially and was just plain down. They laid hands on him and asked that Jesus come into his life. It was the turning point that Jim Ryun had been seeking for years. He had finally discovered real peace.

Jim and his wife went on to have four children. Today, he oversees running camps and trains kids in the techniques he learned on his way to the four-minute mile. He speaks all over the country and world about the most important facet of his life: his faith in Jesus. Running and gold are no longer his gods; Jesus alone is.

Jim was bitter for a long time about the 1972 Olympics and the "foul" that should have been called. But he realized that in Christ all things work together for good, and he believes today that God has used that loss to make a better and greater way.

At the end of his book, *In Quest of Gold*, Jim tells how he and his wife, Anne, walked along the road in Lawrence, Kansas, where they live, and talked about all they had seen and experienced in Jim's stunning career. Anne said, "I praise the Lord that Jesus has never given up on us and continues to mold us into His image."[5]

Jim Ryun continues to be molded into the image of Christ. One day, he can be sure, he will awaken in heaven with that dream fully realized.

---

1. Jim Ryun with Mike Phillips, *In Quest of Gold* (San Francisco: Harper and Row, 1984), 13.
2. Conversation adapted from Ryun, 15–17.
3. Ryun, 18.
4. Ryun, 20.
5. Ryun, 216.

★ Leroy Burrell ★

Height: 5 feet, 11 inches

Weight: 180 pounds

Born: February 21, 1967

Track events: 100 Meters

College: University of Houston

Chapter 3

Leroy Burrell: Breaking Records

While Leroy Burrell knows about frustration, he also knows the exhilaration of victory. He has held the record for the fastest 100 meters in the world twice: in 1991 for only two and a half months, and currently.

Where did this fleet friend of Carl Lewis come from?

Leroy was a shy eight-year-old kid growing up in Lansdowne, Pennsylvania, when his mother left home. Then his father, Leroy Brown, suffered a heart attack and couldn't support the family. Because of this, Leroy went to live with his maternal grandmother, Mrs. Tansy Parns, until he was twelve years old.

Leroy didn't start out a track fan. Instead, he loved baseball. He was thirteen in 1980, when the Philadelphia Phillies won the World Series. In fact, Veterans Stadium, where the Phillies play, stood only fifteen minutes from where he lived.

Leroy wanted to play baseball himself some day, but there was just one problem: He was severely nearsighted in his right eye. When he was younger he was supposed to wear a patch over his left eye to improve the right, but he couldn't see at all that way, so he punched holes in the patch. It helped him see out of his left eye, but it did nothing for his right eye. In fact, today he is legally blind in that eye.

Poor vision is a severe handicap for a baseball player; good eyesight is key to hitting and fielding, if not running. When Leroy went out for baseball, he couldn't see to hit or field. He didn't make the team. But Leroy's coach and homeroom teacher, Bob Kane, cared about this kid who would never play baseball. He said to Leroy one day, "You're a good kid, and I'd love to have you on the team. You can't hit anything, and you can't catch anything. But you're passing people on the base paths. Why don't you go out for track?"[1]

At Penn Wood High School, Leroy signed up for track and immediately became the premier sprinter on the team. But he wasn't only a sprinter. He also performed well in the long jump and the triple jump. His sophomore year he was runner-up in the triple jump at the state meet. Then, during his junior year, he ran on the 4 X 400-relay team that placed second. As a senior he won the state title—by himself. He won the 100 meters in 10.44, the 200 meters in 21.51, the long jump at 23 feet, 4 inches, and the triple jump at 47 feet 3 inches.

Still, it wasn't until Leroy won a scholarship from the University of Houston that he found a coach who could really help him: Tom Tellez. Tellez didn't recruit Leroy as a sprinter, but as a long jumper. He had also coached Carl Lewis, holder of many world records and eight-time Olympic gold medalist. Tellez helped Leroy refine his stride and his posture as a runner with a strict regimen of instruction and workouts. After a short time under the coach's tutelage, Leroy was a world-class long jumper with a best of 26 feet, 9 inches.

Things went well for Leroy in college until the Southwest Conference Championships in 1986. The second he landed in the sand on his second jump, he felt and heard a pop in his left knee—he had torn a ligament. The next day his knee had blown up to the size of a football. Three days later, doctors surgically corrected the problem. But Leroy was on crutches for what seemed like forever. His leg withered, and few people thought he'd ever run again.

Rehabilitation took eight long months. During that time, Leroy did all kinds of exercises, ran in a pool with a flotation device around his torso, and worked out with weights. But even though the injury ended up costing Leroy a whole year of running, something good came out of it: He learned how to focus himself.

The thing Leroy focused on was sprinting. The long jump put too much pressure on his weak left leg, so he put it aside and worked on the 100 and 200. In 1988 he almost qualified for the Olympics, and his confidence soared.

Something else happened to Leroy the next year: He became a Christian. He had been baptized as a twelve-year-old but had never understood the basics of the Christian life or the meaning of walking with Jesus. While at Houston, a campus minister named Sam Mings came by Leroy's room. He asked Leroy, "If you were to die today, are you absolutely, positively certain that you would go to heaven?"

Leroy admitted he wasn't sure. Mings pressed him for a decision, and Leroy finally asked Jesus to take over his life. Later, Leroy said, "It's a blessing that Jesus Christ came into my life. The past four years wouldn't have been so successful. . . . I trust that things will go the way He wants them to go. Some may see it as an excuse, but if things don't go well, then I can easily say, 'That's just the way it's supposed to be.'"[2]

After his years at Houston, Leroy continued running. Racing at an international competition raises big money, as much as $100,000 per man. Carl Lewis commands that much, and Leroy is right behind him. Track and field has become big business—especially when records are at stake.

That was how it was on June 14, 1991, at the USA/Mobil Outdoor Track and Field Championships in New York City. The eight finalists for the 100-meter dash were Carl Lewis, Leroy Burrell, Floyd Heard, Mark Witherspoon, Joe DeLoach, Mike Marsh, Steve Lewis, and Danny Everett. Coming up to the day of the race, Carl Lewis was the world record holder in the 100 with a time of 9.92 seconds. DeLoach had been the 1988 Olympic champion in the 200. Steve Lewis and Danny Everett had finished gold and bronze in the 400 in the 1988 Olympics. It was a formidable crop of runners.

Leroy was coming off the best season of his career. He had won 19 of 22 races, including the Goodwill Games and the Grand Priz finals. Two times he clocked 9.96, the fastest since the 1988 Olympics. He'd also made a mark in the 200, running a wind-aided 19.61, the fastest ever recorded.

The 100-meter dash, for all its shortness, is a grueling race. Just breaking out of the blocks is crucial. Three false starts and you're finished, out of the race. It also takes tremendous training to sprint the entire 100 meters all out. You have to explode upward and outward, then accelerate toward maximum velocity over the next 40 to 60 meters. At 60 meters you peak, and you have to hold that pace or you won't win. The last 40 meters can be very painful as you run all out, every muscle straining for the tape.

Anything can happen at that speed. You can trip over your own feet. You can look to the left or right and lose pace. You can be too tense and tighten up. The 100 can leave you wasted and wrung out, to say nothing of defeated. It's a lot harder than it looks.

As the eight men lined up to run, Leroy felt relaxed. There were many reasons he was the favorite. He'd run the two fastest 100s in the last two years. Carl Lewis was thirty years old and had to slow down sometime soon. Plus, Carl had been off the circuit, promoting his new autobiography and working as sports director on a radio station in Houston—he might be a little out of shape.

The runners slipped into the crouch position. Ready ... Set ... Whoa! Carl Lewis bounded out of the blocks just before the gun sounded. False start. Back to the blocks. Now Leroy knew Carl was nervous and tense and couldn't risk another false start. He'd be cautious. All factors were in Leroy's favor.

Again the runners were called to the line. Ready ... Set ... Bang! Leroy exploded out of the blocks like a volcanic eruption. He got a good start, the best of the field. "I accelerated like I never accelerated before," he remembers.[3]

Leroy reached maximum velocity at 40 meters, and the next 40 meters passed like a dream. Leroy had a full stride on Carl and was leading everyone else. At 80 meters, Leroy suddenly realized where he was, what he was doing. "The race happened so fast. I came to consciousness about eighty meters. It was almost like somebody had pushed fast forward. And I came back."[4]

When consciousness struck, though, Leroy felt he was in the middle of a nightmare. He was dead tired and Carl was gaining on him. The tape was bowed out because of a slight wind. Who would win? Carl actually hit the tape before Leroy did, but Leroy crossed the finish line a foot ahead—in 9.90! A new world record. The pushing wind was clocked at 1.9

miles per hour, just under the 2.0 allowed for world records. The race was legal!

Moments later, reporters crowded around on the infield for an interview. Leroy was close to tears. He said, "When a lifelong dream culminates, you don't know what to think. You imagine yourself feeling very happy, but that isn't exactly what you feel. It's very humbling."[5]

Behind Leroy, Carl had clocked a 9.93, a hundredth of a second over his own just-broken world record.

Two and a half months later at the World Track and Field Championships in Tokyo, Carl Lewis and Leroy Burrell ran against one another again. Some said Carl was definitely getting old and Leroy was the comer, but neither Leroy nor Carl harbored any ill feelings toward each other. They not only trained at the same club, were on the same team, and had the same coach, the two men were also friends and brothers in Christ. Their mothers even sat together in the stands. There was a rivalry, but Carl wasn't out for revenge. He just wanted Leroy and himself to run their best races.

In the quarterfinals, Carl blew by everyone to clock a 9.80. It was the third-fastest time ever recorded in the 100. Because of the wind, however, it was not a world-record time. Carl was still hot in the semifinals, and without the wind he clocked in at 9.93—three-hundredths of a second above Leroy's world record of only a couple months before. Three-hundredths of a second is the blink of an eye, less than a full step in 100 meters. Leroy knew then that his world record was on the line.

Leroy was right behind his friend; he clocked in at 9.94 in the semifinals. Both men were steaming, ready for the finals. So was everyone else: even the emperor and empress of Japan were sitting in the crowd watching.

Leroy took lane three in the finals. To his right in lane four was Linford Christie of Great Britain, who had run a 9.99 in the semis against him. In lane five stood Carl, and next to him in lane six was Dennis Mitchell, also a teammate of Lewis and Burrell. He had also put in a 9.99 showing in the semis.

Mitchell beat everyone out of the blocks, but, after a slight lurch, Leroy accelerated. He felt as good as he had on his world-record run in New York. At 20 meters, four runners took the lead: Burrell, Mitchell, Christie, and Ray Stewart of Jamaica. Carl ran a little behind them. At 60 meters, Leroy had a clear lead—but Carl was moving up. At 80 meters, Leroy and Carl were all out. Mitchell and Stewart were right behind them, less than a footstep away. The crowd leaped to their feet. It looked like the fastest race any of them had ever seen. Records were going to be set!

With 10 meters left, it was Leroy Burrell and Carl

Lewis stride for stride, Leroy on the left and Carl on the right.

But Carl, at six-three, and with his long legs, had an advantage. He could kick those legs out like no one else. Furthermore, Leroy had no idea how close Lewis was because he was blind in his right eye. Then suddenly, Leroy was aware of his friend. He leaned out. 95 meters. Just hairs of a second left on the clock.

And in that instant, Leroy knew it was over. Carl had him. Time: 9.86 seconds. No wind help, either. It was legal: a new world record.

Leroy finished just behind Carl at 9.88, breaking his own record set two months earlier. "My goal was the record," he said. "And I got it. Somebody just broke it a little ahead of me. Who better to lose the record to than a friend you know you can race again."[6]

Meanwhile, Mitchell came in third with a 9.91. The three teammates had taken it, one, two, three. All in all, six men finished under ten seconds. It was the race of the century. And Leroy Burrell had run better than he had ever run in his life.

With the outcome of that race, a rivalry for the new world record, of course, was set. Now Leroy had to beat Carl Lewis's 9.86. Could he do it?

Leroy had his chance at the Athletissima IAAF (International Amateur Athletic Federation) Grand Prix meet in Lausanne, Switzerland, on July 6, 1994.

A slight wind of 1.2 miles per hour was blowing, the same as in Tokyo in 1991. Carl Lewis wasn't there because of a dispute over money (he had wanted $100,000, and the meet committee couldn't go that high).

Leroy ran a 9.85 race, the fastest in history under legal conditions. His teammate Dennis Mitchell and Davidson Ezinwa of Nigeria placed second and third at 9.99. It wasn't the race of the century like the one in Tokyo, but it was a world record. That was good enough for Leroy.

At 27, Leroy Burrell is a powerful force in today's track and field competition. He is also a voice out there, with Carl Lewis, for Jesus. Just like Eric Liddell had been over sixty years before.

---

1. Merrell Noden, "SuperPower," *Sports Illustrated,* 1 July 1991, 49.

2. Ken Walker, "Climbing the Ladder of Success," *Sharing the Victory,* May 1992, 4.

3. Merrell Noden, "Man of the Century," *Sports Illustrated,* 24 June 1991, 34.

4. Noden, 34.

5. Noden, 34.

6. Kenny Moore, "The Great Race," *Sports Illustrated,* 2 September 1991, 26.

★ Dave Johnson ★

USA PACIFIC

Chapter 4

Height: 6 feet, 3 inches

Weight: 190 pounds

Born: April 7, 1963

Track event: Decathlon

College: Azusa Pacific University

Dave Johnson: Mr. Versatility

Not many people follow the decathlon, a sport that involves maximum performance in ten track and field events spread over a grueling two days. That's actually what *decathlon* means: "ten contests." The first day the athlete does the 100-meter dash, long jump, shot put, high jump, and 400-meter run. The second day begins with the 110-meter hurdles, then the discus, pole vault, javelin, and 1500-meter run.

Most track people are specialists who excel at one event—the dash, or the javelin throw, or the discus. Although many try, few people excel in more than one: the competition is just too stiff. In the decathlon, an athlete collects points on the basis of a table established by the IAAF. In recent years, some athletes have topped 8500 points in the event. Presently, Dan O'Brien holds the record: 8891 points.

It takes many athletic skills to win the decathlon: flexibility, endurance, speed, technique, strength. Most of all, it takes focus. That's the way Dave Johnson thinks of it. If he's focused, he has a good chance of performing well. But when he's distracted and worried, hung up on a bad score just finished, or worried about a tough event coming up, he's finished.

Dave grew up in Missoula, Montana. He was not a focused kid. He played a little baseball as a youngster and won some trophies in bowling. But he soon lost interest in sports and started getting into trouble. His parents didn't know how to help him or what to say.

During his teens, Dave drifted more and more. He and a tough group of friends who called themselves the West Side Gang often raided local beer distributors to steal liquor. In the end, Dave was caught several times. He never spent time in prison, but he did have some bad nights in jail. It looked as if Dave's life would comprise little more than run-ins with the law.

Just before his senior year in high school, Dave's father was transferred to Corvallis, Oregon. To meet new people (especially girls), Dave went out for football. He thought he wanted to be a wide receiver. But while he was fast and had good hands, his offensive "moves" were lacking, so he ended up as a kick returner and fourth-string wide receiver.

On the football team, Dave met and became good friends with a third-string wide receiver named Matt Hirte. Matt was a Christian. He didn't pressure Dave about faith, but he was different from most of the other guys; he didn't drink or use drugs. Matt often talked about a personal relationship with Jesus. Dave listened to him, though he made no commitment.

Because Dave was a shy, gangly kid who didn't know how to fit in, drinking had always been his crutch; it was the only way he could overcome his natural shyness. Now in a new neighborhood and not good at making friends, Dave started to get into the party drinking scene.

Dave also got heavily into smoking marijuana. He began feeling nervous and upset under the influence of the drug. One night he was almost killed in a truck wreck on the way home from a party. Miraculously, Dave walked away with no injuries, even after being hurled through the truck window. None of the other four people with him were killed either, but after that Dave gave up smoking dope. He knew it was ruining his life.

In the spring, Dave went out for track. He was the top hurdler and high jumper on the team and ran in the mile relay. The team did well in the district meet that year. Afterward, Dave got a phone call from Dave Bakley, the track coach at nearby Linn-Benton Community College in Albany, Oregon, ten miles from Corvallis. Bakley offered him a spot on the track team if he'd come the next year. He also asked Dave if he'd ever done a decathlon. Dave confused it with the marathon and said he wasn't a long-distance runner.

Coach Bakley explained the difference. He said Dave was just right for the event. If he developed a little muscle, Dave could be good at it. The idea intrigued Dave. It also sounded hard: ten events, seven of which he'd never done before.

Dave greatly appreciated Bakley's phone call. But Linn-Benton had no football team and football was what Dave thought he could build a career on. The next year he decided to attend Western Oregon State where he could play football.

At the same time, Dave was on a spiritual search. His friend Matt invited him to come to a youth group at his church. Dave went and enjoyed it. He became friends with the youth leader, a fellow named Ron, and also another guy named Kurt

Spence. Kurt was kind of a "nerd," but Dave liked him and often questioned him about Christian life and Jesus.

One weekend, Ron took Dave floating on the Willamette River. The long trip exhausted Dave and several times he thought he might drown. Finally, Dave realized Ron might have been trying to "scare" him into making a commitment to Christ by making him think he might die.

Afterward, they both sat down on the bank and prayed. Or rather, Ron prayed. At the end, he opened the time up for Dave to pray too. Dave didn't know what to say. After several uncomfortable minutes, Ron started to end the prayer. But Dave blurted, "Wait a minute, I need to say a little prayer."

Ron waited, and Dave prayed, "Dear Lord, please don't ever give up on me."[1] It was a holy moment. Dave didn't realize it then, but his future path was defined in that instant.

Over the next few weeks, Dave paid much closer attention at youth meetings. He noticed that the Christian kids seemed much freer and more alive than he and his druggie friends. They all had problems; they all struggled with guilt; but they had something else. Dave began to realize that the "something else" was Jesus.

One day at the youth center he told Kurt Spence he wanted to trust Christ. Kurt suggested they take a walk. They went to a nearby park, where Kurt explained what it meant to follow Jesus Christ. Then they prayed. Dave thanked God for loving him and asked for forgiveness of his sins. Then he asked Jesus to take control of his life and help him become what he was meant to be.

It would be great if, from that point on, Dave got it together. But he didn't. He felt a lifting of the feelings of guilt and heaviness, but when he went to college that fall, all the grand dreams he had as a new Christian fell apart.

He started playing football for the junior varsity. He played in every game and hauled in some long bombs, including a TD catch—but he never played varsity. Dave was so angry at the end of the season that he decided to leave Western Oregon the next year.

Dave did stick with track, though, and told the track coach at Western Oregon what Coach Bakley at Linn-Benton had said. He wanted to try the decathlon. The new events were tough, but he improved steadily. He competed in his first decathlon in March 1982 at Willamette University and scored 6297 points. He didn't win, but the leader, a guy named Greg Hanson, scored in the 6800s. It was definitely not a bad showing for Dave's first time out.

Since Dave had made up his mind to leave Western Oregon and he wanted to work on the decathlon, he began thinking about Coach Bakley at Linn-Benton. Finally, he gave the coach a call.

When he asked if the coach remembered him, the answer was immediate: "Of course I do, Dave, how have you been?"

Dave liked the coach's friendliness, his eye contact, and his listening ear. It was clear from the start that the coach was interested in Dave's goals and direction and wanted to help Dave achieve them. Dave decided to go to Linn-Benton the next year.

Dave had a good year at Linn-Benton. He took second place in one decathlon with a score of 6746, and in the NJCAA (National Junior College Athletic Association) national meet, he scored 7225, despite two hurt fingers.

Since Linn-Benton was only a two-year college, Dave had to find another school for his last two years of college. A friend recommended Azusa Pacific University in Los Angeles, California. APU had won the NAIA (National Association of Intercollegiate Athletics) the year before. They had a hot, tough track team. Dave called the coach there, whose name was Terry

57

Franson. A scholarship was worked out, and Dave was on his way.

Dave was soon on target for scoring over 8000 in the decathlon. In fact, that April he did it, at the California Invitationals. The first day Dave set PRs (personal records) in three events: the 100 meters, long jump, and high jump. He also PR'ed in points that day. The second day was even better: he PR'ed in the hurdles, pole vault, and javelin, scoring 8043. He had broken the 8000-point barrier! He had also qualified for the Olympic trials, but he placed eleventh out of fifty-four competitors and didn't make the Olympic team.

After finishing college, Dave continued to train with Coach Franson on his quest to be the best. In fact, he improved to the point that in 1986 he became the best decathlete in America, an incredible achievement for a kid who might have ended up in prison.

Dave had no idea of the problems he would come up against the next year, 1987. A bone spur in his ankle caused him to drop out of one decathlon and miss most of the others. It was basically a lost year. He knew, though, that he had to get ready for the Olympics in 1988. He couldn't afford to have more injuries.

Doctors operated on Dave's ankle and removed the bone spur. But Dave had another injury the doctors didn't know about—a stress fracture in his foot.

Nonetheless, a month before the Olympic trials in July 1988, the pain went away. The bone had actually healed.

At the trials, he scored 8245, third place, less than fifty points out of first place. He made the team for the Seoul Olympics.

Dave had trouble getting focused at Seoul. He made good marks, but less than his personal bests. He ended up in ninth place in the competition with a score of 8180. Christian Schenk of East Germany took the gold with a score of 8488, only 308 points better than Dave. Dave knew he'd be at the Olympics again. And next time, he felt he could medal.

In the years between the 1988 and 1992 Olympics, Dave and fellow American decathlete Dan O'Brien battled it out. Dave signed with Reebok as a sponsor and was able to get some money coming in. Then Reebok began an advertising campaign that pitted Dave against Dan O'Brien. You may remember the TV ads: Who was the greatest athlete in the world? Dave or Dan?

In 1989 Dave almost broke the world record of 8645 set by Bruce Jenner at the 1976 Olympics. Dave scored 8549, only 96 points away. He was number one in the world. Months later, he scored 8600 in the U.S. Championships in Norwalk, California, the second-highest score ever under the present rules and tables. Meanwhile, Dan O'Brien had come in second place, with a score of 8483.

From then on it was a horse race between Dave and Dan. At the Goodwill Games sponsored by the United States and the then Soviet Union, Dave was 300 points behind Dan after the first day's events. The next day, he came up to within 23 points of Dan at the end of the javelin. Only the 1500-meter run, Dan's worst event, was left. Dave blew him away and took first place with a final score of 8403 to Dan's 8358.

In the 1991 U.S. Championships Dan almost broke the world record set by Daley Thompson of Great Britain. He was just three points under it, with 8844, but the score was enough to capture both the number one spot among U.S. decathletes and the U.S. record. Dave came in second with a score of 8467.

At the World Championships that year, in Tokyo, Dan took first place again, scoring 8812, while Dave had to drop out of the competition with a strained knee.

The Olympic trials were coming up. People were still asking who was the greatest—Dan or Dave. It was do or die now.

Two weeks before the trials, Dave was running in training when he felt a strange pop in his foot. There wasn't much pain, but he knew something was wrong. How wrong, he wouldn't know until later.

At the trials in New Orleans, Dave had an average first day while Dan set a world record for first-day points with 4698. The next day, at the end of seven events, Dan was still 500 points ahead of Dave. Could Dave catch up? It was looking like another showdown.

Then in the eighth event, the pole vault, disaster struck for Dan. Both he and Dave had been clearing sixteen feet in practice, but because of injuries earlier in the year, this was the first time Dan had pole-vaulted in a meet. He was nervous.

It showed. In the first attempt, he missed. On the second attempt, he got high enough, but he knocked down the bar. One more miss and he'd be "no-pointed," which meant he'd be out of the running. The pressure was on. Dan ran and planted the pole, but the hesitation was obvious. He didn't make it. Dan O'Brien was off the 1992 Olympic team.

It wasn't over for Dave, though. He cleared over seventeen feet in the pole vault and won the meet with a total score of 8649, his best ever. His second day's performance was also a world-record 4455 points.

The "Who's the Greatest?" Reebok commercials came out saying, "It's Dave." But Dave was a little disappointed. He had liked the friendly competition he'd had with Dan O'Brien—it was a fun, exhilarating rivalry. Now he'd be going to the 1992 Olympics in Barcelona alone.

In addition, the "pop" that Dave had felt earlier while training now became a real problem. Dave's ankle and foot hurt. He spent hours in tests with the doctors, trying to find out what was going on. Soon, the problem was revealed: a stress fracture in the same bone and place in his foot that he'd suffered in 1987. What a time to have such a problem!

The pain didn't get any better. Dave consulted with all kinds of doctors trying to find a way to deal with the pain. He just wanted to compete. He had to compete. Not only for Reebok. Not only for his coaches. Not only for his family or himself. But for his Lord. He wanted his performance in the Olympics to be the height of his career as a decathlete. He hoped a win in Barcelona would allow him to speak for Christ in ways no other platform would allow.

Dave and his coach decided to keep the problem secret, at least from the public. He took it easy, doing only minimal workouts. He did no running. He had to rest.

Finally, they arrived in Barcelona. The morning of the first day's events, Dave got up and gingerly put his weight on the foot. It hurt. He worried about the pain that running 100 meters all out would put on it. He worried about falling in front of millions of people. He worried about letting all his friends, family, and supporters down. And he worried about failing his Lord. He had wanted to be an inspiration to people, but now it looked like it would never happen.

When he reached the stadium, Dave told himself to be careful. Even though his foot was heavily taped, the pain was still there. He couldn't let anyone see he was limping.

Dave started the 100 well; it felt wonderful to let himself go like that again. But halfway through, a stabbing pain erupted in his foot. He felt as if he barely finished the dash, though he clocked an average time of 11.16. He needed to post above-average times and distances and heights to win.

In the long jump, Dave could not warm up as he would have liked because of the rising pain in his foot. He fouled his first attempt. On the second jump, he made over 24 feet. The third jump, he fouled again. He was feeling worse.

Next came the shot put. Dave knew there would be pain in the shot put, but he hoped it would be minimal. He went to the line. There was pain on his push up, pain when he reached to throw the shot, and pain when he stopped himself. He thought it had gone decently, though, until a red flag appeared. He had faulted by touching the toeboard with his foot.

He went through the process again. And faulted again.

Now he was scared. No one faulted three times in the shot put. But here he was, in pain, on the verge of blowing everything.

Dave threw more carefully the third time. He

knew he hadn't faulted. But when he looked up, there was the little man waving the red flag again.

It couldn't happen! No-pointed in the shot put? It meant he would be so far behind in points that he would lose the competition no matter how well he scored in the other events!

Dave was sure he hadn't touched the toeboard. It was a legal throw. He stepped back into the ring. "Hey, come and show me how I fouled," he said to the judge. "Show me what you saw."

The man just stood there, looking confused.

"Do you speak English? Please show me what you saw."

Dave stood there, panicked, terrified, overwhelmed. Had he just blown the whole Games? Had he truly failed? He'd come there with the pain in his foot. He was doing his best. Was it all going to end this way?

Several officials talked together while Dave paced in the shot-put

ring. On the big screens around the stadium, videos displayed what had happened. They went over it several times. Finally, it was agreed: Dave hadn't fouled. But he would have to do it again since they had failed to measure his last shot.

What relief! And hope!

Dave wound up one more time. He threw. And he nailed it: 50 feet, 1 3/4 inches, a personal record, one foot past his best! It was the shot heard round the world.

It seemed like pure luck. Former Olympic decathlete Bruce Jenner even said that to Dave later. But Dave had another idea. The Lord was doing something. A story was about to unfold.

Nonetheless, when Dave came to the next event, the high jump, the crowd booed him. It was rattling and bothersome. Dave knew he just had to gut it out. He kept telling himself that God was doing something through this, but the extreme pain was disheartening. With his foot burning, he was only able to make 6 feet, 3/4 inch.

Finally, at the end of that first day he faced the 400 meters. How could he make that with this pain, and his foot almost crippled? Every step of the race was agony, but Dave kept going. The last 100 meters were the worst. He finished a full second slower than his average.

Still, it was an amazing showing. Here was a man with very nearly a broken foot performing fairly well in one of the toughest competitions any athlete can engage in. The Lord indeed was doing something.

Several reporters had begun to notice that Dave was off and started asking him questions. Dave knew that the secret had to come out soon. He called a press conference and promised to tell the whole story the next morning after the hurdles.

Now Dave had the night to rest. He was in ninth place, 280 points out of the lead. It did not look to be a high-scoring meet, maybe 8600 points at the most. But Dave worried that the pain would only be increased the next day.

Dave slept fitfully and woke up even stiffer than usual. The pain in his foot was tremendous. He didn't know whether he could even walk on it. He felt that all his goals had been dashed to bits. There was no way he could win the gold with his foot like this. He might not even medal at all. Why was the Lord doing this?

But Dave wasn't going to quit now. He had to tough it out. Somehow he had to overcome the pain and hang in there. The first event of the morning was the hurdles. After the third or fourth hurdle, his foot popped again. X rays would show the stress fracture had split even wider. He almost screamed with pain when the pop happened, but somehow he managed to finish with a time of 14.76. It was as if the Lord was strengthening him even as his foot throbbed with agony.

With ice packs on his legs, Dave talked to the reporters. He explained about his foot. They asked a few questions. Soon it was over. No one seemed to be very sympathetic. "Bad break," was about all they could muster.

Limping back to the training room, Dave talked with Coach Franson and a friend named Kevin Reid. He told them he couldn't go on. But they encouraged Dave to keep going. There was no reason to stop now. Both friends felt he could finish. He could still even win the gold! The next event was the discus, which shouldn't hurt his foot much. Why not try?

Dave was skeptical. But he knew they were right. He had to try. For himself. For the U.S.A. For Jesus. He put all of his concentration into throwing the discus and logged an excellent distance of 161 feet. His foot, though, was still in agony. He wondered if he could endure through the next event: the pole vault. So many things could go wrong in the pole vault. So much depended on the performance of that broken foot.

Coach Franson encouraged him to give it a try. "See what happens," he kept saying. Dave wished he would just say, "Okay, drop out," but he wouldn't.

In the pole vault, Dave made it to 16 feet, 8 3/4 inches. But when the bar was raised to 17 feet, 3/4 inch, Dave had to pick up a bigger pole to make it. The weight of the pole and the thought of running harder and faster wore him down. After two failed attempts limping to the line, he threw down the pole in anger. He was through. He stalked out of the stadium.

Coach Franson and Kevin found Dave in the training room. He was crying. He couldn't take any more pain or disappointment. He was through. He had to give up. He couldn't go on for another step.

It was a moment Coach Franson knew would come. He told Dave that he had to finish the meet and leave the rest in God's hands. They hadn't come through eight events to quit now. "Dave, I don't know what the pain feels like," he said. "I know that the emotional pain and everything else has got to be hard for you. But I'm your coach, and I'm saying that we can finish this."

"I don't think so," Dave answered.

"Well, I *do* think so!"

Dave saw the tears in his coach's own eyes. He knew that man loved him and cared about him like a father. And that man also believed in Dave, and in the purpose God had for his life. He put his arms around Dave, and together they cried for a moment.

Dave knew he needed some kind of painkiller to finish. A doctor arrived, checked Dave out, and administered an injection. He had to insert the needle through the top of Dave's foot to get to the bone that had the fracture. The pain of the injection itself was tremendous, but somehow Dave prayed and held on.

He went out to throw the javelin. The pain wasn't reduced at all, it seemed. And his foot felt harder to control. He could barely feel it down there at the end of his leg. He almost fell on the first throw. It landed short.

The partisan crowd, though, was glad. They went on with their cheering and booing like there was no tomorrow.

That in itself was discouraging. But his second throw, far shorter than his best, was good enough to move him from sixth place into third. It was the best he would do that day.

All that was left now was the 1500 meters. Of all the events in the decathlon, that one would be the worst on his foot. But somehow he knew he had to muster the strength to face it.

And do it.

Something happened then that Dave didn't know about until later. Coach Franson had been yelling and cheering from a place in the stands near where Dave threw the javelin. An American boy, about ten or eleven, stopped to talk to Coach:

"Is that Dave?" the boy said.

"Yeah," Coach said. He didn't say more because he was still upset about Dave's situation.

"Dave's gonna win, huh?" the boy said.

"No, I don't think so."

"How come? Isn't he from the Dan and Dave commercials?"

"Yeah, but he's got a broken foot. He broke it just before coming here."

The boy was amazed. "Really? Then what's he doing out there? How can he do that stuff on a broken foot?"

"Because he wants to do his very best. He's an American, and this is the Olympics. He's not going to give up."

The boy stood there as if taking in the meaning of the words. Then he said, "Well, tell Dave to hang in there and give it everything he's got, okay?"

Suddenly, Coach said, "You know why Dave's still out there? Because of little guys just like you. As you get older, you're gonna have times when you want to give up and quit, and that's when you can think of Dave. Remember, don't ever give up, just like Dave isn't giving up. Even though he's not going to win, he's gonna finish because of kids like you."[2]

At the same time, Dave staggered back into the training room. He needed something else for the pain. The last injection hadn't worked. He was completely unprepared for what would happen next. As he lay on the examining table, the doctor jammed the needle right up through his arch. There are few more sensitive parts of the body than the bottom of your foot. The pain was excruciating. Dave couldn't control his tears, or anything else. It all came out. All the pain, despair, and anguish. He had to quit. Coach Franson had to find a way to make Dave keep going:

> "Dave," Coach said, "I think this whole thing is way bigger than you and I even realize. I just finished talking with a boy who thinks you're the greatest thing in the world because you're out there competing with a broken foot." He told Dave about the conversation.
>
> Then he said, "You've got to believe, Dave, that God is allowing an incredible story to unfold through this Olympic Games. It's not the story we thought it would be, and it may not have the same audience you'd have if you'd won the gold medal, with all its glamour and glory. It's really a deep and broad story about lots and lots of people who've stood behind you. It's about a dream, a disappointment, and then about not giving up. You know the Olympics is not really about winning gold medals; it's about that phrase in the Olympic creed: 'Not to have conquered, but to have fought well.'"[3]

Dave pictured Jesus and the pain he went through on the cross. He had been nailed in the foot too. Though Jesus' pain was infinitely greater, Dave realized all that had happened to him was somehow bigger than himself, bigger than his dreams.

He knew Coach was right. He nodded, and then he, Coach, and Kevin prayed together that Dave would have strength for the 1500 meters.

When he stepped off the table, he couldn't tell when his foot had hit the floor.

One more pep talk and Dave limped out the door. The race was called. The decathletes lined up. Dave still couldn't feel anything. It was like he was walking on air with a sudden bump down at the bottom of a pit.

Then the gun resounded. Gritting his teeth, Dave ran 100 meters. Then 200. Then 800. Strangely, the pain diminished. He actually began to speed up.

For the first time in what seemed hours, Dave thought about medals. He knew he couldn't take the gold and probably not the silver. But the bronze was in sight. He had to tough it out as he had a thousand times before. This was against greater odds, greater pain. But God was with him. God could make all things work together for good. He had to keep on.

He finished the race. At the finish, the three medalists were instantly realized. Robert Zmelik of Czechoslovakia won the gold. Antonio Penalver of Spain took the silver. And Dave Johnson of the United States got the bronze.

Dave's heart was full of thanks. He had fought his fight. He had completed his course. He had run his race.

Much more was won that day than a medal. Dave had proven himself as a man who wouldn't quit against towering odds.

His was a faith to marvel at. And an attitude to respect.

You can read more about Dave Johnson in *Today's Heroes: Dave Johnson*.

---

1. Dave Johnson with Verne Becker, *Aim High* (Grand Rapids: Zondervan, 1994), 80.
2. Johnson, 223.
3. Johnson, 224.

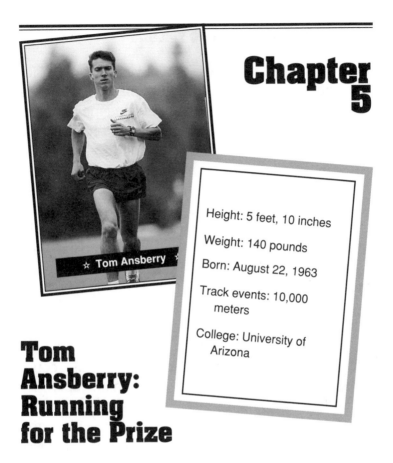

★ Tom Ansberry ★

Chapter 5

Height: 5 feet, 10 inches

Weight: 140 pounds

Born: August 22, 1963

Track events: 10,000 meters

College: University of Arizona

Tom Ansberry: Running for the Prize

Running long distances is painful. Your legs burn. Your gut screams for a rest. Your brain seems on fire. Lactic acid in your legs and arms reaches a crisis point. If you could die at that moment and fly to heaven's arms, you'd be happy.

But you keep going. Why? There are probably as many reasons as there are runners. The Greek soldier who ran from the battle at Marathon in 490 B.C.

to Athens to tell the Athenians of victory ran for life, for truth, for freedom. Others run for a prize. Some run for the sheer pleasure of stretching their body to its limits. Still others run because it's healthy. Or invigorating. Or mentally empowering.

Today, Tom Ansberry of Portland, Oregon, runs for himself, his family, and his Lord. But he also likes to win medals. And he has won many.

Tom began running in Tucson, Arizona, in 1975 at the age of eleven. In fact, he set a record that year by running a 5:03 mile, the fastest mile in his age group in the United States. Then, at thirteen, he went on to run a marathon in 2 hours, 43 minutes. That's a lot of pain and quite an accomplishment!

Tom also had quite a high school career, running both the 1500 and 3000 meters. He was cross-country state champion as a junior and senior. Tom really looked up to his high school track coach and future mentor, Bill Thweatt. "I have a lot of respect for him," Tom says today. "He was a big influence in my life. My parents were getting a divorce at the time, and my dad wasn't around much. Bill became a father figure for me. We spent a lot of time together as he took me to meets, on running trips, and to running camps. He really helped me grow."[1]

Coach Thweatt was also a witness to Tom about Jesus Christ. In fact, he talked to Tom many times. He wasn't pushy, but he often told him about his faith. Tom even started to read the Bible. He made a decision for Christ his first year in college.

"I was reading the Bible a lot and felt convicted," says Tom. "I was going to Coach Thweatt's church, Casas Adobes Baptist in Tucson. One day I heard a message and went forward. It happened that quickly—I was a Christian! I went to that church on and off for five years."[2] The coach and church helped Tom grow both as a runner and as a Christian.

At the University of Arizona, Tom had a track scholarship. He ran the 5000 and 10,000 meters. While in high school the distance races are shorter—the 800, 1500, and 3000—in college they jump to the 800, 1500, 5000, and 10,000. "I was more competitive in the longer distances," Tom says. "I had better endurance than speed, and that's important in longer races."

During his junior year, his best year running, Tom was only fourteen seconds off the best times in the country—college and non-college—in the 10,000. In 1984 he finished second in the Pacific Ten Conference for 5000 meters. In the NCAAs, he finished fourth in the 10,000 with a time of 28:14.8. Tom says, "I was running out of my head. I was running far better than I ever thought I would."[3]

Since he is a Christian, Tom looks at life differently than he would if he didn't believe in Christ. "At one time, running was my whole life," he says. "It was the most important thing to me. Now Jesus is. And my family—my wife, and my daughter, Elyssa. As a runner, you have bad days, bad races. You can get down on yourself and want to give up. But there are many Scriptures that help me see it all in a different way."[4]

In fact, in 1988 Tom went through a real drought. "You know that Scripture—'When He has tested me, I shall come forth as gold'? I feel that God was testing me. You know, would I really stick with it? In 1993 I had to drop out of the U.S. Championships because of injuries. It was a real down time, but I got closer to the Lord and He opened up the right doors. It was like after He tested me, I came back even stronger."[5]

In 1990 Tom was fifth in the U.S. Championships in the 10,000 meters. In 1991 he moved up to fourth. He ran his best 10,000 time ever that year—28:12—at the Mount SAC Relays (Mount San Antonio College). Then, in 1992, he placed fifth in the Olympic trials in New Orleans with a time of 28:48. "I was two places out of making the Olympic team," Tom says. "But I knew I had done my best." It was a disappointment, but it did not keep him from continuing to run and striving for the gold.

Tom likes to strike analogies between the Christian life and running long distance. "When you run races like the 10K, you learn about endurance. It's a daily thing. You train twice a day. Every morning you get up and go out to the track and run whether you feel like it or not. You do the same thing in the afternoon.

"It's the same with a relationship with Christ. You may not feel like getting out of bed and praying, but you have to if you want a relationship with Him. You need to stay in God's Word. You need to spend that time in prayer. It's a daily, everyday kind of thing. It's the only way to build yourself up spiritually. You have to be consistent, like you are in training."[6]

Tom encourages young people who are trying to make it in long-distance running to keep it fun. "My friend and coach, Bill Thweatt, says that today kids aren't as motivated. It's hard to get them to put in the hard work. I never liked some of that hard work either. But I remember how my coach made training and running fun. Running is a very boring thing, just one step in front of the other. All the long distance you do gets very wearing.

"But coach took us on a lot of outings. Camping trips. Sports camps. Overnights. Races in other cities and things like that. He kept running interesting. He made it fun. And as long as it's fun you can keep going."[7]

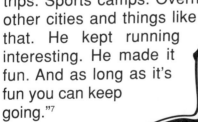

Tom's greatest race came quite

recently, at the 1994 U.S. Championships, when he was 30 years old. Steve Placentia, who was on the Olympic teams in 1988 and 1992, was there. So was Pat Porter, another former Olympian.

"It was hot and humid that day," Tom says, "so I had to be careful. I knew I couldn't run too fast at the start or I would have no energy to finish. The heat and humidity just take the energy out of you. So, when the race started, everybody was holding back."[8]

The pack stayed tightly bunched until the end of 6 kilometers. Then one of the runners broke away from the group. "The conservative pace was over," Tom says. "I knew I had to stick with Steve Placentia or I wouldn't have a chance."[9]

Tom dogged Steve's steps for the next 2 kilometers. Then, at 8 kilometers, Steve moved out ahead. Tom kept right on his heels. "I was there right up to the last 100 meters. Then I started my kick. I moved past Steve and won by about two seconds."[10]

At that point, Tom was the U.S. champion. He went on to the Goodwill Games in Saint Petersburg, Russia, where he raced against the best runners of the 10,000 in the world and placed fourth—a record to be proud of.

While Tom Ansberry does not possess the dashing life history of some of the other runners in this book, he demonstrates the never-give-up spirit of the true athlete. He knows what it is to feel the pain in his gut and keep on going. He knows the hard work it takes to be a U.S. champion. And he knows what it means to walk with Jesus through whatever valleys and mountains he sends your way. As Paul said to the Corinthians, "Do you not know that those who run in a race all run, but *only* one receives the prize? Run in such a way that you may win" (1 Cor. 9:24, NASB). That's what it means to run for the prize. It's what Tom Ansberry has done and will continue to do, both as an athlete and as a Christian.

---

1. Mary Michael, "Running for the Prize," *Sharing the Victory,* April 1991, 17.
2. Michael, 17.
3. Michael, 17.
4. Michael, 17.
5. Michael, 17.
6. Michael, 17.
7. Michael, 17.
8. Michael, 17.
9. Michael, 17.
10. Michael, 17.

☆ Mike Barnett ☆

Chapter 6

Height: 6 feet, 1 inch

Weight: 225 pounds

Born: May 21, 1961

Track event: Javelin

College: Azusa Pacific University

Mike Barnett: Follow Your Heart

The javelin is a spear that weighs 1 3/4 pounds. It's 8 feet, 3 inches long. And people like Mike Barnett run full tilt for 120 feet in order to fling this sharp object anywhere from 250 to 300 feet downfield.

Javelin throwing is not new to history by any means. In ancient Greece, warriors hurled javelins at their enemies to kill them. Athletes threw them for distance, winning a prize for whoever threw the farthest.

Throwing a javelin is a delicate feat that takes both form and strength. If you don't throw with the right form—running, leaping, and throwing—no amount of strength will get you through. However, all the form in the world won't help if you don't have the strength.

Fortunately, Mike Barnett has both.

Mike grew up in California and played football and baseball and wrestled. He was a pitcher and catcher and always had a good arm. He didn't participate in track events until high school, and when he did, he started out as a pole-vaulter. His highest vault was 14 feet, 2 inches—not bad, but not spectacular either.

Mike's brother was a student at Azusa Pacific University and recommended that Mike attend college there after he finished high school. Once on campus, Mike immediately joined the football team. But soon track coach Franson was requiring track practice in the fall, and Mike decided to do track instead of football. One day, while watching some of the other athletes practice, he saw someone throwing a javelin. He thought it looked fun and pretty easy. Even though he had never thrown a javelin before, he decided to give it a try.

Mike walked over to the line and picked up the javelin. Then, without thinking about form, he heaved as hard as he could. He watched, smiling, as the javelin floated through the air for a long ways before coming to the ground. This was the sport for him, he decided.

The APU school record for the javelin was 201 feet, and it had been set two years previously, in 1978. To qualify for the nationals, you had to throw 211 feet. Mike was soon throwing in the low 200s. At a meet at Mount San Antonio College, Mike's first competition throw sailed 235 feet, 10 inches.

That year, Mike won the NAIA (National Association of Intercollegiate Athletics) with a throw of a little over 242 feet. He also qualified to go to the Junior U.S. Championships and was invited to the Pan-American Games in Canada. He won the first with a throw of 228 feet and the second with 236 feet. Seeing the javelin go a little farther each time was a thrill for Mike. Each time he threw, he tried to better his previous mark.

The javelin was not the only sport that Mike excelled at. During his four years in college, he also threw the hammer and the weight. The hammer, which is shaped like an actual hammer, weighs 16 pounds and is attached to a 3 foot wire. On the other end of the wire is a handle. To throw the hammer, you take hold of the handle and start spinning to get up your speed. When you release, the handle, the wire, and the hammer all go flying! The weight is a 35-pound ball that you just heave with all your might. For Mike, the hammer and the weight were pure fun. His best hammer throw was 204 feet, and with the weight, his best heave was 55 feet, 10 inches. That's pretty amazing!

While Mike was working at achieving success in track, God was working on Mike's heart. When Mike started college he had heard a little about Christianity from his brother, who was a new Christian. He noticed a big change in his brother for the better. During his freshman year, Mike continued to hear much more about Christ and what it meant to trust in him through Bible classes and in chapel.

That winter, a friend named David Edsell, who was on both the football and track team, invited Mike to go with him to a party. Mike had a date, so he declined. That same night, David was held up and shot to death by some thugs. When Mike came home, he heard about the shooting. For a moment, he wondered what might have happened to him had he been there too. It scared him. Later that evening Mike reread passages in the Bible and reviewed the *Four Spiritual Laws* booklet. Then he prayed to become a Christian.

Christianity brought some immediate changes into Mike's life. For one, he

86

learned to gain control over his temper. As an athlete, he'd had a do-or-die attitude that often erupted in anger when he lost a contest. After becoming a Christian, he began to realize this was a wrong attitude to have.

Mike also stopped swearing, and sports became less of a controlling force in his life. That's not to say he didn't try just as hard out there—he didn't lose his "killer instinct" or the desire to win—but he did gain a new perspective on sports through his relationship with Christ. And he tried harder to accept both wins and losses as coming from the hand of God.

His sophomore year at Azusa, Mike won the NAIA again. This time he bettered his mark by 10 feet, throwing a little over 252 feet. His junior year, he threw 256 feet, 8 inches, an NAIA record, and his senior year he won one more time with a throw of 256 feet, 10 inches, beating his previous record by 2 inches. Excited, Mike began thinking seriously about the 1984 Olympics.

He threw well at the trials—258 feet—but he was number ten on the list. He wouldn't be going to the 1984 Olympics. It was a disappointment for Mike. He stopped competing and put his equipment aside. He got married, moved, and started a business. But then, in 1987, he got the bug again. He wanted to try for the 1988 Olympics.

That year, Mike won the U.S. Championships and competed in the World Championships in

Rome, taking fourth place with a throw of 258 feet, 10 inches. Now he was confident he could make the Olympic team.

At the Olympic trials in 1988, everything went perfectly. Mike was in third place till the very end of the competition. Then the unexpected happened: The very last competitor, with his very last throw, blew everyone away. That athlete won the competition and knocked Mike into fourth place. Once again, he would not be able to realize his dream of competing in the Olympics, though he was an alternate.

In 1989, Mike won the U.S. Championships again, with a throw of 256 feet, 8 inches. He then travelled to the World Cup in Barcelona and took fourth place, throwing 256 feet, 3 inches. It seemed he couldn't get beyond that 256-feet mark.

The next year, Mike took third in the U.S. Championships and was an alternate for the Goodwill Games, missing second place by only 2 inches. He was disappointed again, but he wasn't going to give up.

In 1991, he again won the U.S. Championships with a throw of 262 feet. He went to the Pan-American Games in Cuba that year and took second place. Then it was on to the World Championships in Tokyo where he performed miserably and ended up in twenty-fourth place. It was disappointing, but Mike had his best throw ahead of him. He flung that spear 276 feet, 4 inches at the Sports Festival in Santa

Barbara. Encouraged, Mike set his sights on the 1992 Olympics.

In the 1992 Olympic trials Mike finally made the Olympic team. A goal he'd had for thirteen years was coming true: He was going to Barcelona as the number-two javelin man in America! He was 32 years old.

Mike arrived in Spain on July 10. He roomed with Brian Crouser, a friend of several years who was also a javelin thrower and who had been on the 1988 team. On the qualifying day for the javelin, 47 athletes participated. Each athlete got three throws; the twelve with the longest throws would make it to the finals. Mike's goal was simply to make it into the final twelve who would compete for the bronze, silver, and gold medals.

There was some real excitement in the qualifying round. Throwers were lining up. Mike's first throw of 259 feet, 7 3/4 inches gave him a good placement. Slowly but surely, though, he slipped back as others made better throws. His heart was pounding. Then, on one of the final throws, someone nearly matched his distance with a throw of 259 feet, 7 inches. Mike had kept twelfth place by only three-quarters of an inch! He would go on to the final round.

The day of the finals, the stands were packed for the 400-meter run and the 4 x 100 relays. Over 60,000 people were watching in person, to say nothing of the people all around the world watching on TV.

"I felt much more relaxed than I expected," Mike says. "It was exciting, but I wanted to compete and do well. I'd made the final cut. Now all I wanted was to do my best. I realize now that if I had made the 1984 or 1988 Olympic team I would have folded up. I wasn't ready back then. The Lord needed to do some work in me to prepare me for this experience. I was glad I had hung in there and kept trying all those years."

Mike stepped up to the line, ran the 120 feet to the tape, and threw. His distance was actually shorter than his throw had been in the qualifying round. But it turned out to be the best of his three attempts: 258 feet, 7 inches. Good enough for seventh place.

"It was a great moment," Mike says. "All those people watching. It was the most exciting meet I've ever been in. I remember coming in during the opening ceremonies—just walking along the track. I thank the Lord he kept me going all those years. I might have given up after 1984, but he stirred me up in 1987 to keep training. I might have given up after 1988, but I was doing better than ever so I kept on. Who knows, maybe I'll even make it to the 1996 Olympics! The world record, though, is over 313 feet. Some Czech guy. That will be hard to beat. He's been undefeated in 55 straight meets. But I'd still like to be there."

These days, Mike spends his time working on his

business, training, and being a husband and father of two kids, Cory, eight, and Shawna, four. "If God wants me to do great things with the javelin," says Mike, "then he'll do it. I don't worry about that anymore."

What advice does Mike give to aspiring throwers of the javelin?

"Get around you people who can build you up," he urges. "Don't listen to people who tell you you can't do it or that you aren't good enough. If you train hard enough, have the right motives, put together attainable goals, and don't quit, I guarantee you'll do well. Follow your heart."

That's good advice for any sport, any dream. Follow your heart and your Lord, and you won't get off the track.

All quotes for this chapter come from the author's personal interview with Mike Barnett.